I0806717

EVERYTHING SPORTS

EVERYTHING SOCCER

SYDNEY NEWTON

A Crabtree Canopy Book

Crabtree Publishing
crabtreebooks.com

EVERYTHING SPORTS

Author
Sydney Newton

Contributors
Amanda Bishop
Sarah Dann
Jennie Haw

Editors
Sissy McGonagal
Crystal Sikkens

Proofreader
Melissa Boyce

Design
Margaret Salter

Production manager
Candice Campbell

Images
Alamy: p. 24 (top), p. 26 (middle), p. 44 (bottom)
Newscom: p. 26 (bottom) Tony Quinn; p. 36 (both) Bildbyran; p.37 (bottom left) Howard C. Smith
Wikimedia Commons: p. 6 (bottom); p. 7 (inset); p. 8 (top left and bottom); p. 9 (top right); p. 11 (all); p. 12 (middle, and bottom), p. 14 (all); p. 15 (top); p. 16 (all); p. 17; p. 19 (logos); p. 22; p. 23 (top, middle, bottom left); p. 24 (bottom); p. 28 (middle and bottom); p. 30 (bottom); p. 30 (top middle); p. 31 (right insets); p. 37 (top right); p. 38 (bottom) cristiano barni; p. 40 (top and bottom); p. 41 (both); p. 42 (top); p. 43 (top); p. 44 (top); p. 46 (middle image and middle inset); p. 47 (bottom); p. 49; p. 50; p. 51 (bottom right); p. 53 (top right); p. 54; p. 55 (bottom left); p. 56 (bottom); p. 57 (top); p. 61 (top)
Shutterstock: p. 1 Victor Velter; p. 5 (middle) p. 10 (top left), 55 (top right) Marco Iacobucci; p. 7 (bottom) Stray Toki; p. 9 (bottom) Ian Francis; p. 12 (top) Janmarie37; p. 13 (top) Kostas Koutsaftikis; p. 13 (bottom) mooinblack; p. 18, 20, 31 (bottom), p. 33 (bottom) A. RICARDO; p. 21 (top) Ringo Chiu; p. 21 (bottom) Denys Rudenko; p. 23 (bottom right) Nick N A; p. 25 (top) Carlo Kaminski; p. 25 (middle) fifg; p. 25 (bottom) Vladimir Melnik; p. 27 (middle) Jose Breton- Pics Action; p. 28-29 lazyllama; p. 30 (top left) supawat phunkhan; p. 30 (top right) Tony Baggett; p. 32 (top and bottom) Marco Ciccolella; p. 34-35 (bottom) Vitalii Vitleo; p. 35 (inset) Howard Cheng; p. 38 (top left) Cosmin Iftode; p. 39 ACHPF; p. 45 (left) Marcos Mesa Sam Wordley; p. 45 (right) cristiano barni; p. 46 (top) Focus Pix; (bottom inset) Maxisport; p. 47 (top) Ververidis Vasilis; p. 48 beltsazar; p. 51 (top right) Romain Biard; (bottom left) feelphoto; p. 52 (left and right) Paolo Bona; p. 53 (bottom) 360b; p. 55 (bottom right), p. 58, p. 60 ph.FAB; p. 56 (top) artnana; (middle) rook76; p. 57 (bottom) Maxisport; p. 59 Jan van Dasler; p. 61 (middle) Kathy Hutchins; p. 61 (bottom) Dorothy Hong; front cover Mikolaj Barbanell
All other images: Shutterstock.com

Crabtree Publishing

crabtreebooks.com 800-387-7650

Copyright © 2026 Crabtree Publishing

All rights reserved. No part of this publication may be reproduced, stored in a retrieval system or be transmitted in any form or by any means, electronic, mechanical, photocopying, recording, or otherwise, without the prior written permission of Crabtree Publishing.

In Canada: We acknowledge the financial support of the Government of Canada through the Canada Book Fund for our publishing activities.

Hardcover 978-1-0398-7488-6
Ebook (pdf) 978-1-0398-8176-1
Epub 978-1-0398-8296-6

Published in Canada
Crabtree Publishing
616 Welland Avenue
St. Catharines, Ontario
L2M 5V6

Published in the United States
Crabtree Publishing
347 Fifth Avenue
Suite 1402-145
New York, NY 10016

Library and Archives Canada Cataloguing in Publication
Available at the Library and Archives Canada

Library of Congress Cataloging-in-Publication Data
Available at the Library of Congress

Printed in the U.S.A./CP072026

CONTENTS

INTRODUCTION

WORLD OF SOCCER

Soccer is one of the world's most popular sports. It is played and celebrated all around the world in international, national, and local leagues. **It is also widely enjoyed as a recreational sport.**

One of the reasons for soccer's popularity is how simple it is to play. It can be played by anyone, and almost anywhere. All you need to play is a ball and two goal markers. Players who do not have a ball can **improvise** and make a ball using socks, coconuts, or even scraps of fabric tied together.

Soccer has been called "the beautiful game," "the king sport," and "the world game."

Clubs and Leagues

There are many **professional** soccer or association football leagues around the world. They all follow the Laws of the Game—a set of rules originally set down in 1863 to uniformly regulate soccer throughout the world. Most leagues fall under the Fédération Internationale de Football Association (FIFA), which is the international **governing body** for soccer. FIFA has six confederations, or groups, that organize soccer events throughout the world for men's and women's league teams. FIFA events include Gold Cup competitions in North America, Champions League in Europe, and FIFA Club World Cup, as well as many others.

Every four years, FIFA organizes a tournament called the World Cup where the best teams from countries around the world play against one another.

FAST FACT

FIFA is also the governing body for beach soccer and futsal. Futsal is a soccer game played on an indoor court.

What's in a Name?

In most of the world, soccer is referred to as "football" but, in the United States, Canada, and Australia, it is called soccer. The rules of soccer were set by England's Football Association in 1863. "Association Football" spread quickly around the world. "Association" was soon shortened to "assocer" and then to simply "soccer." Because North Americans also play a version of **rugby** football known simply as football, association football is commonly known as "soccer" in North America.

CHAPTER 1

SOCCER HISTORY

Soccer has a very long and global history. One of the earliest soccer-like games was played in early China (255–206 B.C.E.). "Tsu-chu," also called "cuju," was played with a leather ball filled with feathers and hair. To score, players kicked the ball through a hole in a cloth stretched between two poles.

Ancient Greek and Roman soldiers played their own version of soccer to develop their agility and speed. Although these games provided exercise and training for soldiers, they were also a form of entertainment. Many people liked to watch the games and cheer on the different teams.

FAST FACT

In many countries, a soccer field is known as a pitch.

Ancient Chinese soldiers played tsu-chu as part of their training.

What's in a Name?

The Greeks called their game "episkyros," or game, and the Romans called it "harpastum," or ball. In both games, players kicked a small ball across a field, trying to get the ball across the opposing team's boundary lines to score. The teams were much bigger than they are today, with 27 players on each team.

The Aztecs (1200–1500 C.E.) played a game called "tlachtli" that combined soccer and basketball. To play, two teams moved a ball across the field without using their hands or letting the ball touch the ground. Players tried to pass the ball through a stone ring on the opposing team's side. The first team to score was the winner.

Kemari is an ancient kind of soccer that is still played today at festivals in Japan. Players pass the ball to each other and try to keep it in the air as long as possible.

Mob football was so violent that people living nearby would barricade, or block, their windows during matches.

Mob Football

Early soccer-like games were very violent. Players could do anything—including punch, kick, and wrestle—to get the ball from another player. Known as "mob football," these games were **chaotic**, with no formal rules, no restrictions about who could play, and no limit to the number of players on the field. They were usually played in the country, but sometimes they were played in towns. Excited fans and players caused a lot of property damage, which upset many people.

Too Much Football!

In 1349, England's King Edward III complained publicly about his soldiers spending too much time playing "football." By this time, soldiers did not need to be as quick on their feet—it was more important that they be good **marksmen** rather than fast foot soldiers. Playing kicking games was no longer considered important training for soldiers.

Centuries-Old Match

The Royal Shrovetide Football match occurs annually in the town of Ashbourne. It has been played since at least the 12th century. The two teams that play are called the Up'Ards and the Down'Ards.

The ball used in England's Royal Shrovetide Football match is larger than a standard soccer ball. It is hand-painted and filled with Portuguese cork so it will float in the water.

The British "handling game" of football developed into rugby.

British Growth

Soccer continued to grow in popularity, especially in England. By the 1500s, many students were playing games of football at school. By the 1800s, there were two different types of British football. In the "handling game," players pushed and **tackled** to get the ball. They could catch the ball with their hands and run with it. In the "dribbling game," players couldn't tackle each other or touch the ball with their hands.

The "dribbling game" later became today's game of soccer.

Referees are officials that make sure the rules of soccer are followed. In 1581, a teacher named Richard Mulcaster was one of the first people to encourage the use of referees because of the game's violence.

Early Rulemakers

As football became more popular, teams from different schools and clubs needed rules to follow when competing. In 1863, Ebenezer Morley established the Football Association (FA) to govern and regulate football. The FA was made up of representatives from different schools across England. The members agreed on the first set of soccer rules in London in 1863.

Colonel Nathaniel Cresswick

The world's first football club was the Sheffield Football Club, founded in 1857 by two British army officers, Colonel Nathaniel Cresswick and Major William Priest.

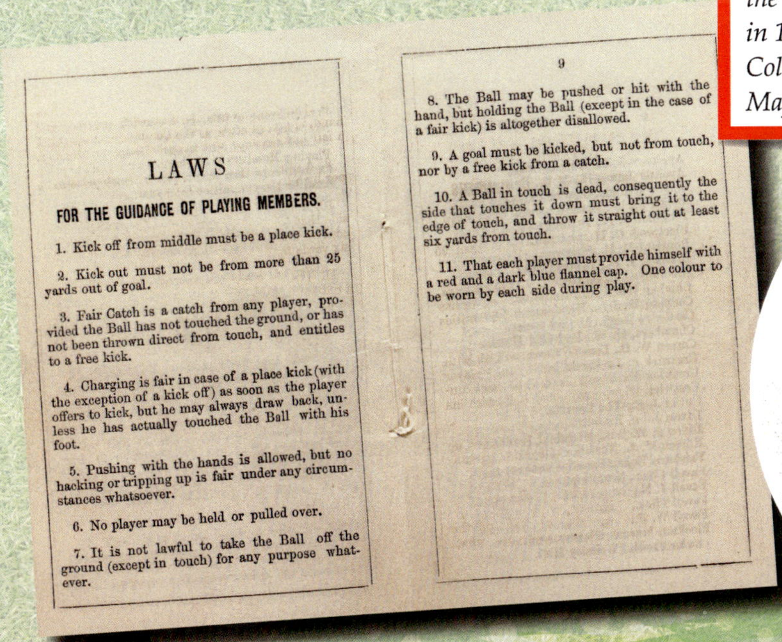

LAWS

FOR THE GUIDANCE OF PLAYING MEMBERS.

1. Kick off from middle must be a place kick.

2. Kick out must not be from more than 25 yards out of goal.

3. Fair Catch is a catch from any player, provided the Ball has not touched the ground, or has not been thrown direct from touch, and entitles to a free kick.

4. Charging is fair in case of a place kick (with the exception of a kick off) as soon as the player offers to kick, but he may always draw back, unless he has actually touched the Ball with his foot.

5. Pushing with the hands is allowed, but no hacking or tripping up is fair under any circumstances whatsoever.

6. No player may be held or pulled over.

7. It is not lawful to take the Ball off the ground (except in touch) for any purpose whatever.

9

8. The Ball may be pushed or hit with the hand, but holding the Ball (except in the case of a fair kick) is altogether disallowed.

9. A goal must be kicked, but not from touch, nor by a free kick from a catch.

10. A Ball in touch is dead, consequently the side that touches it down must bring it to the edge of touch, and throw it straight out at least six yards from touch.

11. That each player must provide himself with a red and a dark blue flannel cap. One colour to be worn by each side during play.

Major William Priest

The Game Spreads

English sailors who spent months at sea would jump at the chance to play a quick match, or game, of "football" when they went ashore in other countries. Local people in these countries saw them playing and began to play themselves. Soccer soon spread around the world.

The Beautiful Game

In South America, football began as a sport played by wealthy individuals. However, by 1914, it had spread to poorer neighborhoods and kids began playing games in the streets. Today, many South American countries are known for their very talented soccer players.

A new style of football emerged on the streets of Brazil. Brazilians are known for playing with greater speed, style, and skill than many European players. They use their chests to bring the ball to the ground and move the ball quickly with their feet. Many fans consider the Brazilian style to be the most beautiful kind of football to watch.

Brazilian soccer superstar Edson Arantes do Nascimento, known as Pelé, is regarded by many as the best player of all time. He was the all-time leading scorer of the Brazilian national team and a national hero.

Pelé died in 2022 at age 82. Hundreds of thousands attended his wake and funeral, which began at a soccer stadium.

Soccer in Asia

In the late 1800s, British **colonists** brought association football to countries in Asia. Football grew significantly in the mid-1900s in countries such as Korea, China, India, and Japan. South Korea's national team is considered to be one of the top Asian football teams. The team played in its first Olympics in 1948 and its first World Cup in 1954.

Since 1986, South Korea has played in every World Cup tournament.

In North America

Soccer traveled across the ocean to North America in the late 1800s. British businessmen introduced football at Harvard and other colleges. Early leagues usually used the name "football" and games were played with 25 players on each side. However, at that time, college students were already playing rugby or an early form of American football. They were not interested in playing a "kicking game" using FA rules. The game then moved into working-class communities where interest quickly grew. By the early 1900s, many major American newspapers began calling the game "soccer."

Harvard vs. Yale.

Foot Ball Match.

HAMILTON PARK,

Saturday, Nov. 13th, 1875.

Tuttle, Morehouse & Taylor, Printers, New Haven.

The Fall River Rovers were one of the first soccer clubs in the United States.

"Canadian Rules"

The first football match between a British team, the Pilgrims, and a Canadian team, the Berlin Rangers, was held in 1904. The British players were surprised to learn that Canadian teams played by "Canadian Rules." These rules allowed players to be more physical, meaning players could trip each other. The Canadian team beat the British 2–1. The British team complained about their aggressive playing. However, by 1908, the "Canadian Rules" were replaced as Canadian teams began to follow traditional FA rules.

In Canada, soccer was still commonly called football until about 1945.

Post-War Influences

After World War I (1914–1918), many people from Britain moved to North America. This helped encourage the growth of soccer. However, during World War II (1939–1945), many players went overseas to fight and many football organizations in North America closed down. After the war, football had to be rebuilt.

Open for Women

With the FA rules in place, soccer became much safer for players. Most players were male, since football was played in all-boys schools and men-only club teams. However, the FA rules made it easier for women to play, and many did.

*The Dick, Kerr Ladies FC was formed in 1917 during World War I by female workers at a **munitions** factory.*

In 1920, 53,000 fans watched a charity soccer match between the Dick, Kerr Ladies Football Club (FC) and the St. Helen Ladies team in Liverpool.

Afterward, the FA banned women from playing on their fields. Some people believe that the popularity of the women's game upset the men of the FA. The FA did not lift their ban until 1971.

Paid to Play

Although club football games were very competitive, FA rules did not allow players to be paid to play. In 1882, the FA learned that Scottish players on the Blackburn Rovers team were being paid. The FA declared that the payment must stop. The Blackburn Rovers didn't want to lose players who couldn't afford to play without earning money. They threatened to leave the FA and start their own league if the FA did not change the rule. The FA decided to make the change so that teams were allowed to start paying players—and professional football was born!

BLACKBURN ROVERS, 1884-5, 1885-6.

CHAPTER 2

FIFA'S IN THE GAME

The Fédération Internationale de Football Association (FIFA) was formed in 1904. FIFA is a federation of national soccer associations. Its headquarters is located in Zurich, Switzerland.

FIFA is a self-governing association. The member associations of FIFA all agree to play soccer using the same regulations, or rules. FIFA also organizes international tournaments such as the World Cup. Today, FIFA has 211 members—more members than the United Nations!

FAST FACT

FIFA's founding countries were France, Belgium, Denmark, Netherlands, Spain, Sweden, and Switzerland.

Six Confederations

FIFA's national associations are part of six **continental confederations**. The Asian Football Confederation (AFC) represents Asian and Australian nations. The Confédération Africaine de Football (CAF) represents African nations. The Confederation of North, Central America and Caribbean Association Football (Concacaf) represents North American, Central American, and Caribbean nations. Confederación Sudamericana de Fútbol, or CONMEBOL, represents South American nations. The Oceania Football Confederation (OFC) represents Oceanian nations. The Union of European Football Associations (UEFA) represents European nations.

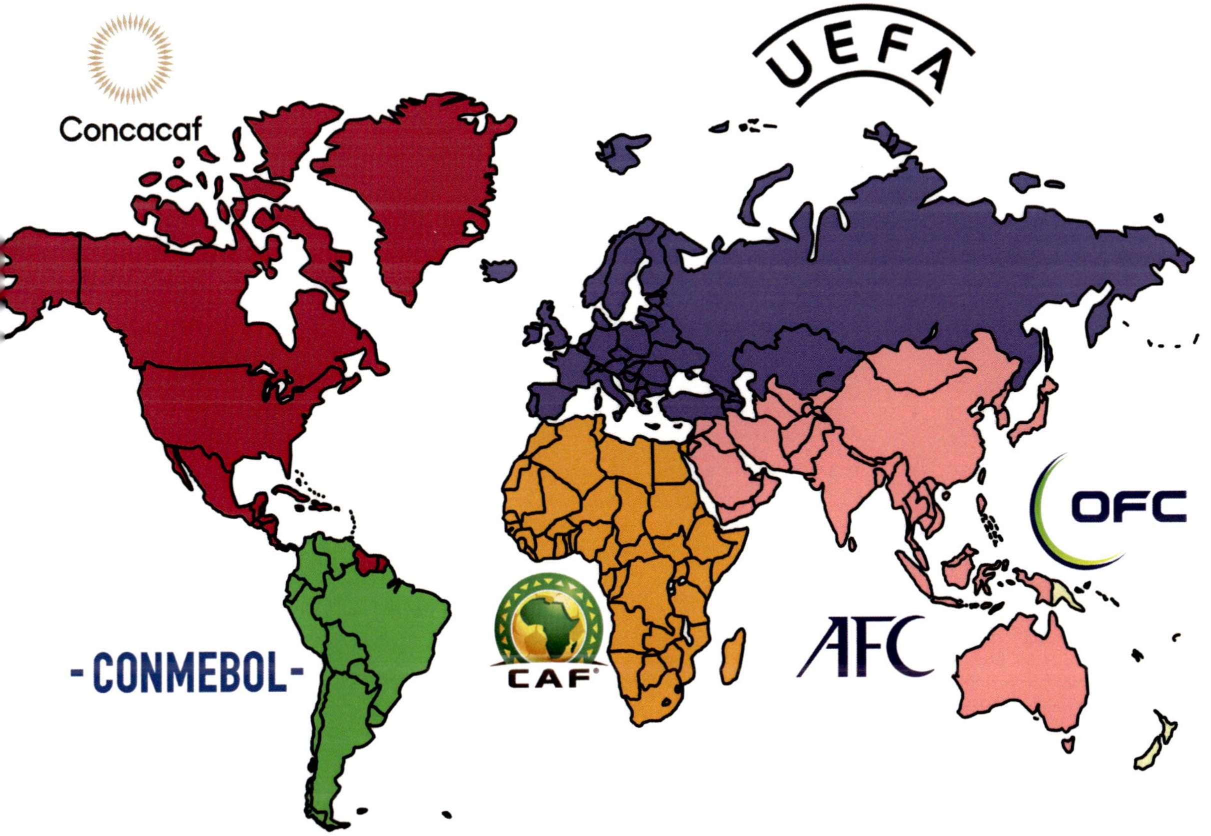

Confederations Cup

Confederations host tournaments for their member teams. A **qualifying event** decides which teams move on to the next level of competition. The Confederations Cup was an event held every four years from 1992 until 2017. Eight teams competed for this title, including the top team from each confederation, the World Cup championship team, and a team from the host country. It was originally a tournament held in Saudi Arabia called the King Fahd Cup, after the Saudi ruler who helped organize it. It was held just before the World Cup. FIFA ended the tournament and replaced it by expanding the World Cup.

Brazil won the Confederations Cup four times, making them the most successful team in the tournament's history.

Qualifying for World Cup

To qualify for the FIFA World Cup, national teams must play and rank in tournaments organized by the six FIFA confederations. FIFA decides the number of places in the finals that each zone gets. This is based on the number and strength of teams in each confederation's qualifying tournaments.

Concacaf, for example, holds several tournaments including the Gold Cup men's championship, the W Gold Cup for women's national teams, as well as league and premier club tournaments. The Concacaf Champions Cup, formerly the Champions League, is a competition where champions automatically qualify for the FIFA World Cup.

The Concacaf Gold Cup trophy is about 26 inches (66 cm) tall and weighs around 20 pounds (9 kg).

The Canadian women's national soccer team secured their spot at the 2024 Paris Olympics and Women's Gold Cup when they defeated Jamaica at the the Concacaf Olympic play-in series.

First FIFA World Cup

The first FIFA World Cup competition was held in Uruguay in 1930. The World Cup, like the Olympics, is held every four years. FIFA chose Uruguay as the host country for that first Cup because its team had won the gold medal in both the 1924 and 1928 Olympics. Teams were invited to play, instead of qualifying as they do today. Only four teams from Europe agreed to go, because sailing to South America for the tournament required teams to be away from home for more than two months! The final number of participating teams was 13.

When Uruguay beat Argentina in the final match to win the very first Cup, a national holiday was declared!

Uruguay Wins!

At the first tournament in Uruguay in 1930, Uruguayan player Héctor Castro inspired the world. Castro had lost his arm when he was only 13, but it did not stop him from playing soccer. He went on to score Uruguay's first goal in the World Cup, as well as the last goal in the final, winning the first World Cup for the host country.

Jules Rimet Trophy

Trophy

The Jules Rimet Trophy was awarded to the World Cup winner until it was permanently given to Brazil in 1970 after their third World Cup victory. It was stolen in 1983 and never found. From 1974 to present day, the FIFA World Cup Trophy has been used. The $20-million trophy was last awarded to Argentina in 2022.

FIFA World Cup Trophy

More Firsts

The first African team to make it to the World Cup was Egypt in 1934. Then the world had to wait until 1970 to see another African team play in the tournament. In 1986, Morocco became the first African team to make it to the second round. Then in 1990, Roger Milla of Cameroon made a brilliant steal from his Colombian opponent during extra time in a group-stage game. He brought the ball down the field and scored. Cameroon won the match and became the first African team to make it to the **quarter-finals**.

Milla scored four goals during the 1990 FIFA World Cup. At the age of 38, he became the oldest goalscorer in World Cup history. He broke his own record four years later when he scored at the 1994 World Cup at the age of 42.

Morocco was the first African team to make it to the ***semi-final*** *round of the World Cup in 2022. They lost to France, who in turn lost to Argentina in the Cup final.*

First in South Africa

The 2010 World Cup in South Africa was the first to be held on that continent. In 2007, 204 men's teams began competing to qualify for one of the 32 available World Cup spots. Each of the 32 qualifiers received \$1 million from FIFA to help pay for training in preparation for the tournament. Teams were also awarded prize money. The winning country, Spain, received \$30 million in addition to the Cup! Spain defeated the Netherlands 1–0 to win, and Germany beat Uruguay 3–2 in the third-place game.

The 2010 World Cup became known for the loud sounds of fans blowing the vuvuzela, a long plastic horn with a big noise.

The World Cup is a major and massive sports event that earns billions of dollars in ticket and merchandise sales, as well as broadcasting rights, sponsorships, and hospitality.

Zakumi was the mascot for the 2010 World Cup.

Women's World Cup

In 1991, China hosted the first FIFA Women's World Cup. National teams from 49 countries competed to make the top 12 and play in the final tournament. Sixty-five thousand people filled the stands to watch the final match. The United States claimed victory when they defeated Norway 2–1 for the Cup. Sweden beat Germany 4–0 in the third-place game.

At the 1991 Women's World Cup, the players were not the only history-makers on the field. For the first time in FIFA history, female officials took to the fields to call the shots!

Qualifying for the Cup

To qualify for the Women's World Cup, teams battle it out in FIFA continental zone tournaments. Before these tournaments, FIFA decides the number of spots for each continental zone. This is based partly on the strength of the teams.

As with the men's World Cup, the host nation's team automatically qualifies. Held every four years, the Women's World Cup is the major event in women's association football. The United States women's team has won the most World Cups, followed by Germany.

Japan became the first Asian team to win a World Cup after beating the United States in a shoot-out in the final game of the 2011 Women's World Cup.

Soccer Leaders

The United States women's team has long been a leader in international soccer. After winning the first Women's World Cup in 1991, they won again in 1999, 2015, and 2019. They won Olympic gold medals in 1996, 2004, 2008, 2012, and 2024. The team has won the **Algarve Cup** ten times to date!

CHAPTER 3

OLYMPIC SOCCER

The first soccer tournaments at the Olympic Games were held in 1900 and 1904. They were men-only events, with women's soccer only being added to the Olympics in 1996.

While the International Olympic Committee (IOC) recognizes the 1900 and 1904 Olympic soccer competitions as official tournaments, FIFA does not. At the 1908 Summer Olympics in London, a recognized international tournament took place. In the final match, Britain beat Denmark 2–0 to win a gold medal. The win came as a surprise, as Denmark had won their semi-final match with France 17–1!

The first Olympic soccer tournament in 1900 was held in Paris, France. The Games returned to Paris in 1924 and 2024.

Adjusting the Rules

Until the 1980s, Olympic soccer rules stated that players must be **amateurs**. But in 1984, the IOC decided to allowed professional players to compete. FIFA did not want Olympic soccer to compete with its tournaments. The IOC and FIFA compromised. Since most of the world's top soccer players were from Europe and South America, FIFA adjusted the rules.

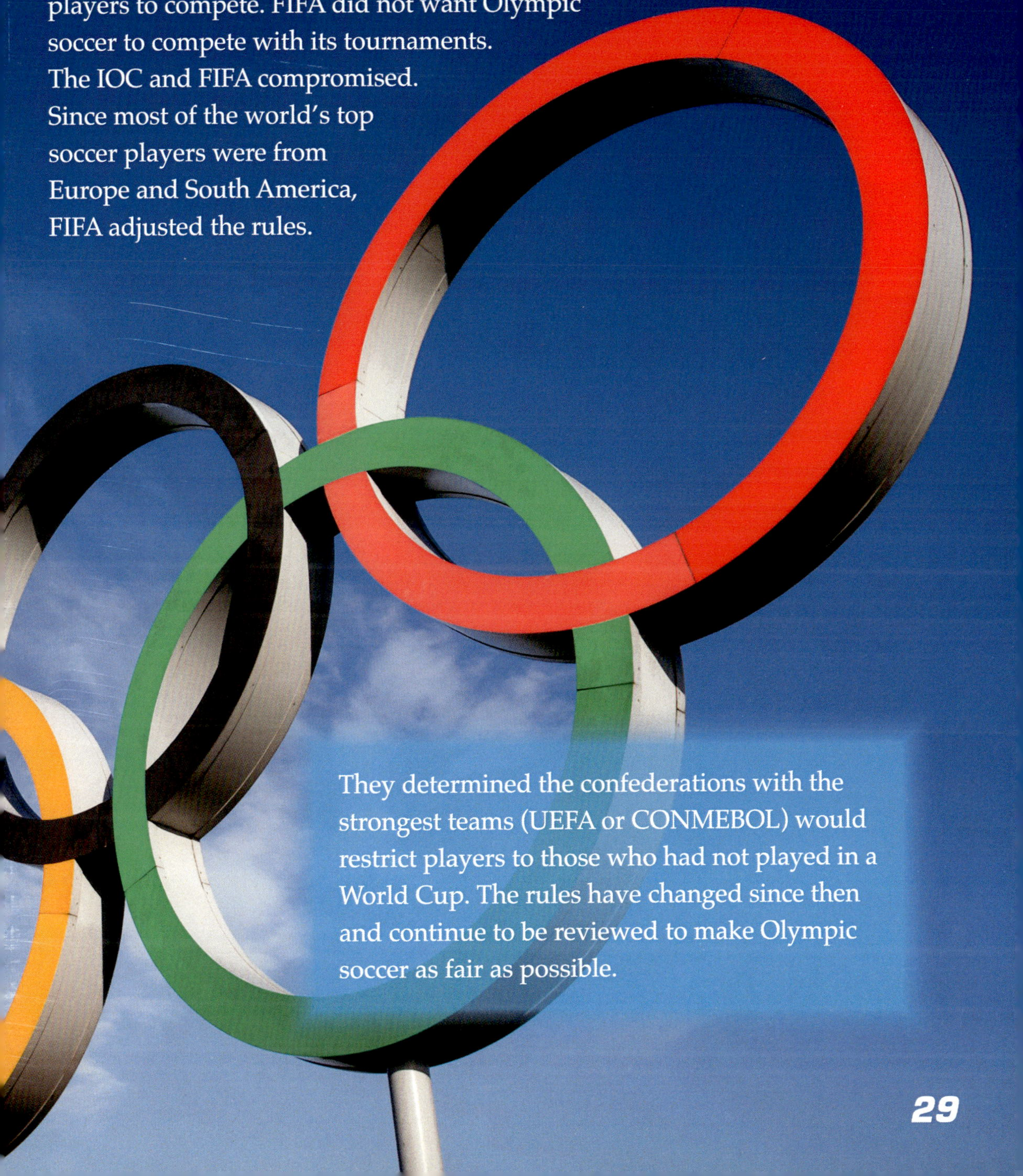

They determined the confederations with the strongest teams (UEFA or CONMEBOL) would restrict players to those who had not played in a World Cup. The rules have changed since then and continue to be reviewed to make Olympic soccer as fair as possible.

FAST FACT

Team USA's Christie Rampone is the top Olympic soccer medal winner with three golds and one silver.

Women's Olympic Soccer

After 96 years of men's Olympic soccer, women's teams were finally allowed to compete at the 1996 Olympics in Atlanta, Georgia. Soccer had been played by women for more than 100 years, but opportunities for women to play on the world stage were rare until recently.

The top eight teams from the 1995 Women's World Cup qualified for that first Olympic appearance. With a home-field advantage, the U.S. women's team won the first-ever women's Olympic gold medal in soccer in front of a stadium packed with fans. The United States women's team has won the most Olympic golds.

Women's Olympic soccer has helped build the sport's reputation and popularity. It helped women's soccer become the fastest-growing sport in the world by the mid-2020s. Superstars such as Cristiane Rozeira de Souza Silva and fellow Brazilian and Olympic teammate Marta Vieira da Silva have changed the way fans view the sport. Top American Olympians Abby Wambach, Mia Hamm, and Megan Rapinoe are household names. Canadian Olympic soccer hero Christine Sinclair is third in all-time Olympic scoring and teammate Melissa Tancredi ranks in the top 10. Top women's Olympic players also play in professional leagues around the world. Until 2022, the U.S. women's national team was paid less than players on the men's team. That year, they reached an agreement with their governing body, the United States Soccer Federation. The $24-million settlement included an agreement for equal pay for both women's and men's national soccer teams and equal working conditions.

Christine Sinclair

Melissa Tancredi

The U.S. women's team is a gold-medal powerhouse.

Paralympic Games

The Paralympic Games are an international sporting event for athletes with disabilities. They are held every four years, shortly after the Olympics have ended. There are two kinds of Paralympic soccer: seven-a-side and five-a-side.

Seven-a-Side

Seven-a-side soccer was part of the Summer Paralympic Games from 1984 until 2016. It is played on a smaller field but follows the same rules as regular soccer with some changes. There is no **offside** rule and players can take **throw-ins** underhand or with one arm. Athletes who play seven-a-side soccer have **muscular impairments** resulting from **cerebral palsy**, strokes, or brain injuries.

The 2020 Summer Paralympics took place in Tokyo, Japan.

Five-a-Side

Five-a-side soccer is played by athletes who are **visually impaired**. The goalkeeper can be fully sighted, but the other four players must wear blindfolds to make sure that they all have the same level of visual impairment. A guide behind each team's net yells directions to help players when they are trying to score a goal. The ball used to play the game has a bell inside to help the players follow it. A **rebound** wall keeps the ball on the field and there is no offside or throw-ins in the game. Five-a-side soccer for the visually impaired started in Spain during the 1920s, and the first international tournament was held in 1998 in Brazil. The game was featured for the first time as a Summer Paralympic sport in Athens, Greece, in 2004.

Brazil (green and white) won five consecutive gold medals in five-a-side at the 2004 to 2020 Summer Paralympics.

CHAPTER 4

EUROPE AND AMERICA

Football, le foot, fútbal, calcio, soccer—whatever name you call it, it is the most-loved sport in Europe. It is more popular than any other, with dozens of national football associations and top-playing and top-paying professional leagues.

Europeans are wild about soccer. They play it, watch it, and argue with each other about it. Founded in 1954, the Union of European Football Associations (UEFA) is the governing body for soccer in Europe. It was started as a way to strengthen the sport after the destruction and bleakness of World War II. UEFA is also a confederation under FIFA, soccer's world-governing body.

UEFA has 55 national football associations as members. It organizes championships for men's and women's adult and youth teams throughout Europe. These include the UEFA European Football Championship, also known as "the Euro." The men's and women's Euro tournaments take place every four years, and pit the best European teams against one other.

Women's Euro

The first Women's Euro was held in 1991 with four teams in competition. By 2013, the Women's Euro had expanded to 12 teams. The spectacular 2013 event set records in attendance. One of the biggest surprises was the Danish team, which made it all the way to the semi-finals without winning a game in regular time! In the end, Germany took home the gold medal after defeating Norway. More than 41,000 fans cheered on their teams at the final game! In 2017, the Women's Euro expanded to 16 teams. Germany ended their 22-year reign as champions of Europe when they lost to Denmark in the quarter-finals. Host-country the Netherlands took home their first gold medal as they defeated Denmark in the final.

FAST FACT

The first men's Euro was held in 1960 in France.

In 2022, host-country England took home their first gold medal and were declared champions of Europe.

Teamwork

Over the years, Euro tournaments have showcased some heart-stopping moments filled with amazing plays and terrific teamwork! Euro 1992 had it all. The men's team from Denmark did not even qualify for the tournament. They were added only after Yugoslavia had to leave the tournament. Denmark surprised everyone by beating the Netherlands in penalty kicks to win the semi-final game. When Denmark defeated Germany to win the Cup, sports fans all over Europe could barely believe it!

Denmark had less than two weeks to prepare for the tournament.

Denmark beat Germany 2–0 in the Euro 1992 final. This was their first European title.

Golden Goal Rule

The following year, FIFA introduced the rule of the golden goal, or the first goal scored in overtime to immediately end the game. Euro 1996 was the first to allow the golden goal. In the final match between Germany and the Czech Republic, Oliver Bierhoff leveled the score at 1–1 during regular time. Then, in the fifth minute of extra time, or the overtime period, he scored again to win and end the game.

German striker Oliver Bierhoff scored the first golden goal in a major tournament. The golden goal was dropped from the Laws of the Game in 2004.

Marianne Pettersen

Norwegian striker Marianne Pettersen first played for her national team in 1994. She later scored one of the two goals that led Norway to victory over Germany in the 1995 Women's World Cup. But in Norway's opening game against Denmark at the Women's Euro 1997, Pettersen scored a whopping four of the team's five goals to beat Denmark 5–0! Norway did not advance out of the group stage, but it was an unforgettable performance from a top player.

Each team in the Premier League plays 38 games, with seasons running from August to May.

The Big Leagues

In UEFA-governed professional soccer, five "big leagues" dominate. These leagues have the top talent and make the most money. They include the Premier League in England, Bundesliga in Germany, La Liga in Spain, Serie A in Italy, and Ligue 1 in France. Each country operates its own league, with teams ranked in divisions according to performance.

Premier League

Premier League soccer is the world's most-watched league. Fans all over the world watch Premier League matches on television. Matches attract more than 40,000 spectators, and 20 clubs compete.

The Premier League is linked to the the English Football League (EFL) through an open-league team promotions system. The EFL is the oldest football league in the world, with three divisions: the Championship, League One, and League Two. These have 72 clubs.

Founded in 1898, Serie A is the highest level of the Italian football league system.

North American Leagues

Major League Soccer (MLS) is the men's premier professional soccer league in the U.S. and Canada. Thirty teams compete—27 in the U.S. and three in Canada. Teams compete in a season from February until October, with championship tournaments, or playoffs, in November. The MLS Cup is the end-of-season championship game. The winner of the MLS Cup—for both Canadian and American teams—is awarded a berth in the next season's FIFA Concacaf Champions Cup.

The National Women's Soccer League (NWSL) was formed in the U.S. in 2012 as a successor to Women's Professional Soccer and several previous women's pro leagues. The 16-club league is a member of Concacaf and includes players from the U.S., Canada, and other nations.

The Northern Super League is a professional women's soccer league in Canada. It played its first matches in 2025 with six founding clubs.

CHAPTER 5

SOCCER SUPERSTARS

Soccer's superstars are the very best players in the game. Their abilities and performance on the field set them apart. Top club teams are packed with stars brought in from all over the world. When star players appear on their national teams in international tournaments such as the FIFA World Cup, the home crowd goes wild!

Edson Arantes do Nascimento, better known as Pelé, was one of the best male soccer players in history. He first caught the world's attention at the 1958 World Cup at age 17. The Brazilian forward made history by scoring a hat trick, or three goals in one game, in the tournament and becoming the youngest player ever to win a World Cup! He went on to play and win two more World Cups.

*As a forward and **attacking** midfielder, Pelé scored almost 1,300 goals in his career!*

Mia Hamm

Mariel "Mia" Hamm is known as one of the best female soccer players of all time. She joined the U.S. national women's team at age 15. She was only 19 when the team took home the first Women's World Cup in 1991. As a forward, Hamm was a top goalscorer. After retiring in 2004, she still held the record of 158 international goals until 2013. Even one of the greatests thought she was a greatest! In 2004, Pelé chose Hamm as one of two women on his list of top 125 soccer players for FIFA's 100-year anniversary. Hamm coached and wrote books in retirement before becoming the co-owner of the Los Angeles MLS team and serving on the board of the National Soccer Hall of fame.

Fantastic Forwards

Forwards tend to be some of the fastest players on the team. They need to be able to run around the other team's players to get into position to score goals. Some of the best soccer forwards are strikers who have out-of-this-world physical and technical skills. They are accurate kickers with a superior ability to find their way past the defense and take shots on goal. They play as far forward on the field as they can get without being called offside. If they can hit their target when it counts the most, forwards can become national heroes!

FAST FACT

The Ballon d'Or, or Golden Ball, is an award presented by *France Football* magazine to top male players as chosen by soccer journalists. Forwards are often top picks.

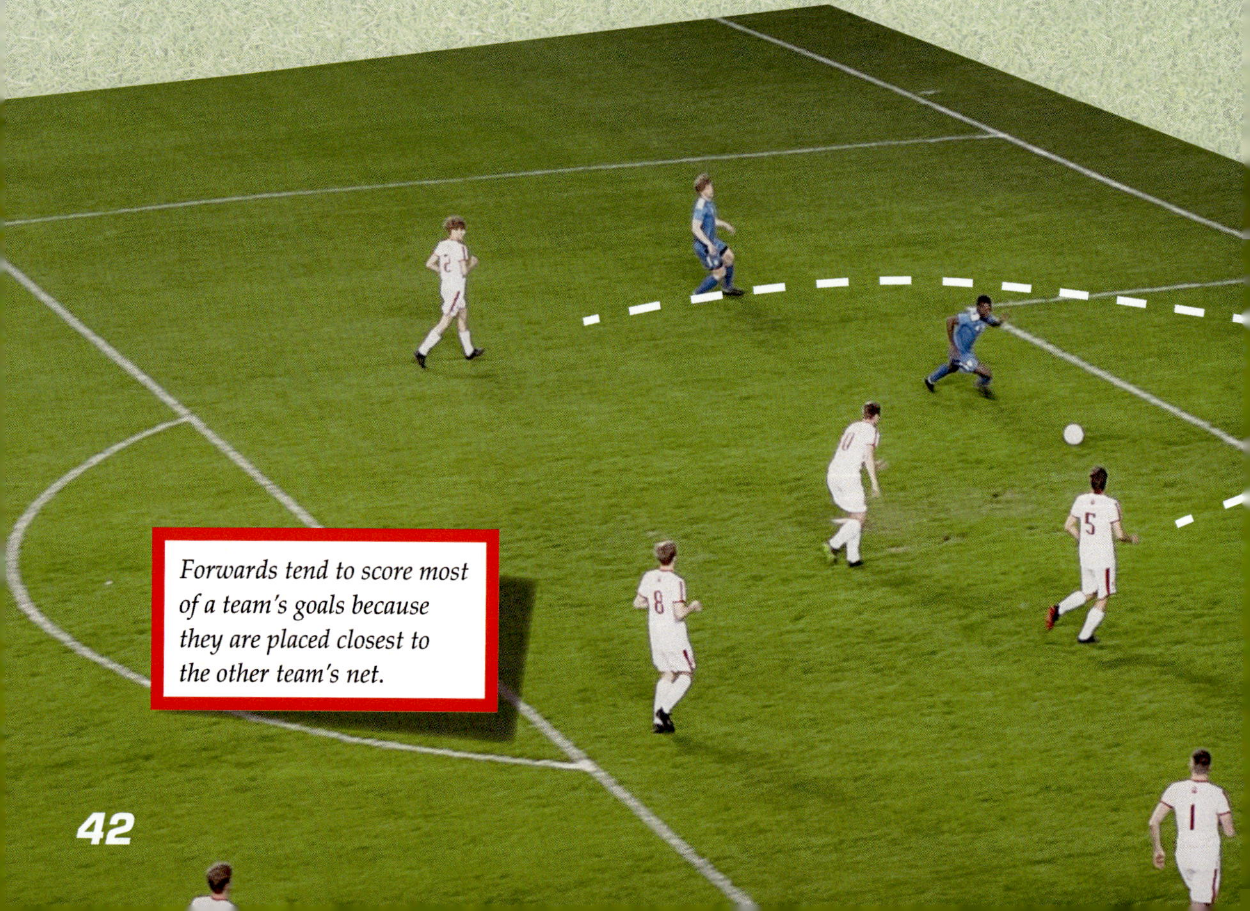

Forwards tend to score most of a team's goals because they are placed closest to the other team's net.

Ronaldo

One of the greatest soccer forwards of all time, Ronaldo Luís Nazário de Lima, is, like Pelé, known by his first name. Born and raised in Brazil, he dropped out of school at 12 to play soccer. A top striker, champion dribbler, and clutch player, Ronaldo became FIFA World Player of the Year three times and was inducted into three soccer Halls of Fame.

Injuries forced Ronaldo to retire. In retirement, he became majority owner of Real Valladolid Club de Fútbol. He also bought the club he played for as a young boy.

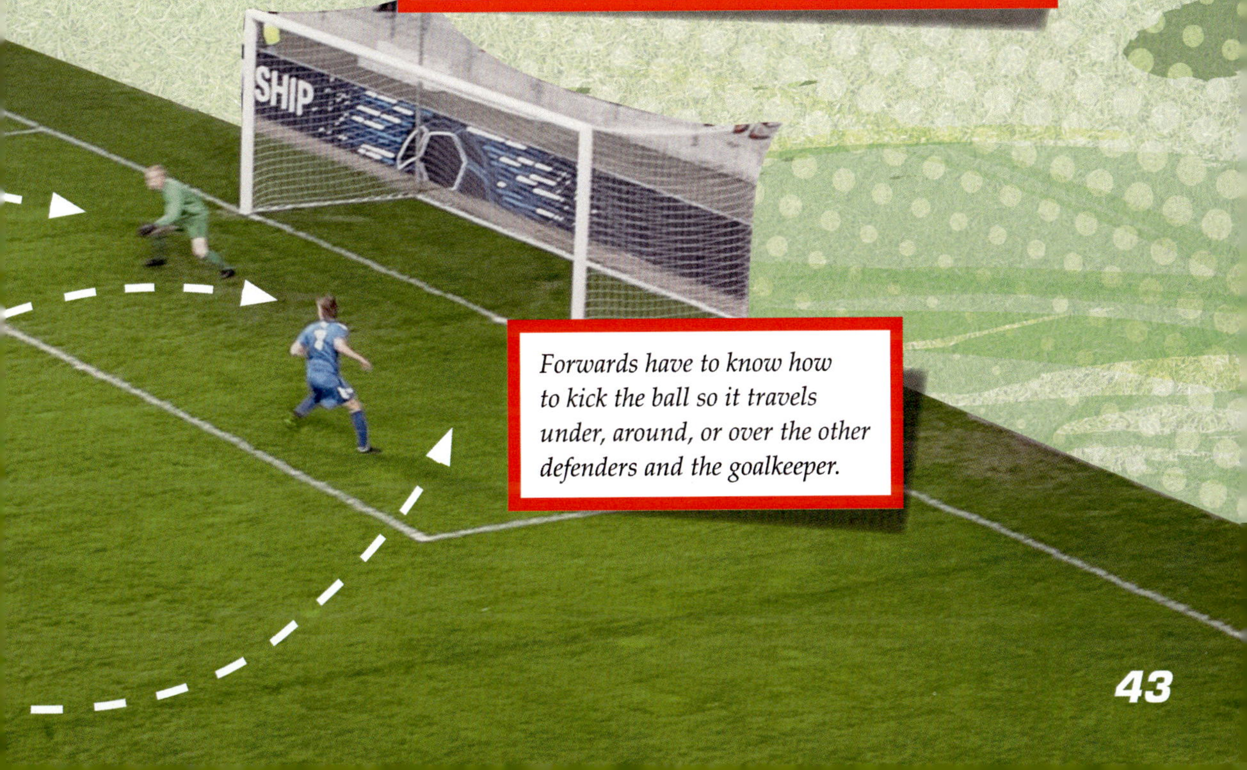

Forwards have to know how to kick the ball so it travels under, around, or over the other defenders and the goalkeeper.

Abby Wambach

American forward Abby Wambach first played for the U.S. women's national team in 2003. In her 13-year playing career, she won one Women's World Cup and two Olympic gold medals (2004 and 2012). Wambach has also played in all three women's leagues created in the United States since 2001. She was named the U.S. Soccer Federation's Female Athlete of the Year six times between 2003 and 2013.

Wambach's goal in the 122nd minute of the quarter-final match at the Women's World Cup in 2011 set a record for the latest goal ever scored during World Cup play!

The Other Ronaldo

Portugal's Cristiano Ronaldo has won dozens of awards for his achievements on the field, including the FIFA World Player of the Year in 2008. In 2009, he became the most expensive soccer player in history and ranks as one of the world's highest-paid athletes. Ronaldo has played for club teams in Portugal's Primeira Liga, the Premier League, La Liga, and the Saudi Pro League. In 2011–2012, he set a La Liga record by scoring at least once against every opposing team in one season.

Ronaldo holds the record for top goalscorer of all time, having scored over 970 official senior career goals for club and country.

Marta became the first player, male or female, to score in five different World Cups and five consecutive Olympics.

Just Marta

Many people believe that Brazilian striker Marta Vieira da Silva, known simply as "Marta," is the best female soccer player in the world. She was FIFA's World Player of the Year six times, winning every year from 2006 to 2010 and again in 2018. Marta has played in leagues in Brazil, the United States, and Sweden, and has played in five Women's World Cups and five Olympic tournaments. At the 2007 World Cup, she was awarded both the Golden Shoe and the Golden Ball awards.

"Leo" Messi

Quick-footed Lionel Messi is the captain of Argentina's men's team and the MLS Inter Miami team. Many believe he is the greatest player on the field today. In 2005, he was the FIFA U-20 top goalscorer and player of the tournament. Three years later, he won Olympic gold with Argentina. Messi played for FC Barcelona for 17 seasons and won a club-record 34 trophies. In 2013, Messi improved on Ronaldo's La Liga record by scoring on every team in consecutive games during one season.

Messi has won eight Ballon d'Or awards and a record six European Golden Shoes. In 2022, he won his first FIFA World Cup.

Maradona

Argentina's Diego Maradona is known for scoring one of the worst and one of the best goals in World Cup history within moments of one another. In the 1986 quarter-final match against England, the English goalkeeper came out to punch a ball clear of the net. Maradona knocked the first goal in with his hand, which the referee did not see. The English team protested the goal, but the call stood. A few minutes later, Maradona scored again by dribbling past five English players in what was later called one of the greatest goals of the century.

Midfielders

Midfielders are often the most **versatile** players on a team. They can fall back to help the defense and shoot forward if they see a chance for a goal or an **assist**. Midfielders manage the play by spotting opportunities, controlling the game's pace, or speed, and knowing when to make a move.

David Beckham

England's David Beckham may be soccer's best-known player today. He was a strong midfielder known for long-range goals, especially from **corner kicks**. He won titles in four different soccer leagues—the Premier League, La Liga in Spain, the Major League in North America, and Ligue 1 in France. He captained the English national team for six years. Beckham is well known as a celebrity. He retired as a player in 2013 and became part-owner of Inter Miami.

Beckham is the first English footballer to win league titles in four different countries–England, Spain, the United States, and France.

Homare Sawa

Midfielder Homare Sawa was only 15 when she made her first appearance for the Japanese national team. She went on to play in four Olympic tournaments and six Women's World Cup tournaments. She captained the team for their 2011 World Cup victory. She scored five goals in the tournament, won the Golden Ball as top goalscorer, the Golden Shoe as top player, and was named FIFA Women's World Player of the Year. After retiring from international competition, she returned to play for her Japanese league team, INAC Kobe Leonessa.

After placing second in the 2015 Women's World Cup, Sawa announced her retirement from international competition for the second and final time.

Yaya Touré

Hailing from Côte d'Ivoire (Ivory Coast), Yaya Touré was one of soccer's top midfielders. He often changed position during games, and was known for his speed and creativity in making goal-scoring opportunities. Touré played in Belgium, Ukraine, Greece, and France before joining FC Barcelona in 2007. He also played alongside his brother, defender Kolo Touré, for FC Manchester City. The two brothers were a part of the Côte d'Ivoire national team in the 2006, 2010, and 2014 World Cup tournaments.

Touré retired from international football in May 2019. He went on to pursue a career in coaching, including an assistant coach position for Saudi Arabia's national team.

Megan Rapinoe

American midfielder Megan Rapinoe is known for her clever on-field moves—and her long career. She played in U-16 and U-19 tournaments, including the U-19 Women's World Championship in 2004. She played in the 2011 FIFA Women's World Cup, where the U.S. took home silver. In the next two World Cup tournaments in 2015 and 2019, she helped the U.S. team win gold. She also won gold in the 2012 Olympics and bronze in 2020. Rapinoe received the Presidential Medal of Freedom in 2022, and retired after the 2023 World Cup.

At the 2019 FIFA Women's World Cup in France, Rapinoe was awarded the Golden Shoe and Golden Ball awards.

Using His Head

Midfielder Jone Samuelson of Norway broke records when he headed a ball 190.7 feet (58.13 m) up the field—right into the opposing team's empty net!

Dynamic Defenders

The best defenders are fast, sharp, and fearless. It is their job to stop attacks from the opposing team and to keep them as far from the net as possible. They must make good tackles and strong passes to move the ball up the field. Many are good scorers as well.

Il Capitano

Italy's Paolo Maldini was one of soccer's best defensive players. Nicknamed "Il Capitano," or "The Captain," Maldini was known for his size, strength, and leadership. When playing, he tried to tackle as little as possible. Instead, he positioned himself on the field to stop attacking players. He played for Serie A team AC Milan for his entire career.

AC Milan retired Maldini's jersey, number 3, in 2009.

Faye White

Faye White of England joined the national team at age 16. She went on to captain the team at four major international tournaments. To this day, she is the longest-serving female captain of England. She also played for Arsenal Ladies FC in the Women's Premier League from 1996 to 2013. As team captain, White led Arsenal to 15 major championship titles.

In honor of her outstanding achievements, White was inducted into the English Football Hall of Fame in 2015.

Der Kaiser

Legendary German defender Franz Beckenbauer is regarded as the greatest German soccer player of all time. Nicknamed "der Kaiser," or "the Emperor," he was named European Footballer of the Year twice. Beckenbauer was known as a sweeper, a defender who plays behind the other defenders and blocks any gaps. After retirement, he worked as a commentator and helped bring the 2006 World Cup to Germany. When Beckenbauer died in 2024, his memorial service was held in a soccer stadium.

Philipp Lahm

At 5 feet 7 inches (1.7 m) tall, Philipp Lahm demonstrated that defenders don't have to be giants to be superstars. His speed and agility, as well as his ability to play both sides of the pitch, helped him stay with the ball and slow down attacking forwards. He was the longtime captain of Bayern Munich of Bundesliga. At his first World Cup in 2006, he scored the first goal of the tournament. In 2010, he became the German national team's youngest captain ever.

Lahm led Germany to win the 2014 FIFA World Cup. Afterward, he announced his retirement from international football.

Captain Kompany

Belgian center-back Vincent Kompany started playing for his national team and the Belgian Pro League when he was only 17 years old. In 2008, he moved to Manchester City FC in the English Premier League. Kompany was voted the team's Player of the Year for the 2010–2011 season. The next year, he was named Player of the Season for the entire Premier League. He became captain of the Belgian national squad and led them to two World Cups in 2014 and 2018. Kompany completed a Master of Business Administration degree before retiring, and went on to a career in team management.

Kompany became manager of the Premier League club Burnley before moving to Bayern Munich as coach.

Top Defenders

Germany's Lothar Matthäus (left) and Italy's Fabio Cannavaro (right) are the only two defenders to have won FIFA's World Player of the Year award.

Great Goalkeepers

Great goalkeepers never take their eyes off the ball. They see everything on the field and react. The best keepers are ready to stretch, dive, or leap across the goal to keep the ball out of the net.

Black Spider

Lev Yashin was born in 1929 in the former Soviet Union. He was nicknamed the "Black Spider" because he always dressed in black and seemed to have extra arms when making saves. He was one of the first keepers to punch the ball away instead of always trying to catch it. With three World Cup appearances and a 1956 Olympic gold medal, he was named the best goalkeeper of the 20th century by the International Federation of Football History and Statistics (IFFHS).

Yashin had 270 career shutouts, or games with no goals allowed.

Hope Solo

American Hope Solo began playing forward on her high school soccer team. She switched her position to goalkeeper at the University of Washington. Solo was keeper for leagues in Sweden, France, and the United States. She also played with the United States national team from 2000–2016. In 2013, Solo joined the Seattle Reign FC in the National Women's Soccer League. She won Olympic gold twice and appeared in two World Cups.

In 2015, Solo helped the United States win their third FIFA World Cup.

Iker Casillas

Iker Casillas was the captain of Spain's winning team at the 2010 World Cup, where he won the Golden Glove for best keeper of the tournament. He also won the Golden Glove after Spain's 2008 and 2012 Euro victories. Both FIFA and IFFHS named him the world's best keeper from 2008 to 2012.

CHAPTER 6

STARS OFF THE FIELD

Not every soccer superstar is known for dribbling, shots, and saves. Coaches, managers, trainers, and officials all have important roles to play. Many of the people who help make soccer great work on the sidelines, behind the scenes, or in soccer club offices.

Soccer officials have to stay in great physical shape. Referees must know all of the rules, and be ready to make judgment calls in tricky situations. Pierluigi Collina of Italy was a fair and effective referee. Before he retired at the age of 45, he had officiated final matches at the Olympics, the Euro Cup, and the World Cup.

The International Federation of Football History & Statistics named Collina the World's Best Referee six years in a row from 1998 to 2003.

Total Footballer

Johan Cruyff is considered a game changer. The Dutch player and manager is credited with bringing Total Football to the main stage of the pro leagues. Total Football is a system of playing that makes all players adaptable to different roles. An outfielder can take over the role of any other player: attacker or defender. Cruyff used it when he was both a player and a manager. As a player for clubs including Ajax and Barcelona, he was known as a fast and agile dribbler. As a manager, he focused on training, awareness, and building skills for seamless plays. He was also known for his one-liners, such as "If I wanted you to understand it, I would have explained it better." Cruyff set up a foundation to help disadvantaged children. He died from lung cancer in 2016.

Ajax fans erected a statue of Cruyff in front of the Amsterdam stadium in 2020.

Spectacular Fans

Soccer fans are an important part of the game. They passionately support their teams and buy tickets and merchandise that boost team revenues. Some fans also have a reputation for being too passionate and taking their team rivalries too far. Soccer hooliganism, violence, and rioting was a major problem until clubs and FIFA started clamping down. Fan bases can also do good. Brazilian soccer fan Silvia Grecco won the FIFA Fan Award in 2019. She was honored for narrating, or match reporting, all the moves of the Palmeiras (São Paulo) football club for her blind son.

Don Carlo

Player, coach, manager—Carlo Ancelotti has done it all with flair and substance. Ancelotti began his playing career as a midfielder in 1974 for Italian Serie C team Parma. He was transferred to Roma in 1979 and then to AC Milan from 1987 to 1992. He was also on the Italian national team for the 1986 and 1991 World Cup. Don Carlo, as he was nicknamed, retired at 33 due to injury and began a new career as coach. He coached four Italian clubs, including AC Milan in 2007 when they won the UEFA Super Cup and FIFA Club World Cup. Ancelotti went on to coach or manage more powerhouses, including Chelsea FC of the English Premier League, Real Madrid, and Brazil's national team. Ancelotti was at the helm as manager for five UEFA Champions League finals wins and has won the World Cup three times.

Ancelotti was the head coach of Real Madrid when the club won the 2024 UEFA Champions League final.

Stéphanie Frappart

Stéphanie Frappart was the first woman to referee a major European men's match in 2019 and a men's FIFA World Cup in 2022. She has also been an official in UEFA Champions League and UEFA Women's Champions League matches, as well as the Women's Euro 2025 final.

Star Owners

Who owns professional soccer teams? Investment companies, wealthy families, fan trusts, and...movie and music stars! It costs millions to own a club, so many have multiple owners. Celebrities are the newest group to buy into soccer teams. They bring followers and fans and help promote and make money for the teams through their high profiles. In 2021, actors Ryan Rynolds and Rob McElhenney bought Wrexham AFC in Wales for $2.5 million. They turned the third-oldest football club in the world into National League champions—and they made a television show about the club! Other celebrity soccer club part-owners include actor Matthew McConaughey (Austin FC), tennis legend Serena Williams (Angel City FC), and rappers Drake (AC Milan and Venezia) and Snoop Dog (Swansea City AFC), among others.

Matthew McConaughey

Serena Williams

GLOSSARY

Algarve Cup A women's annual international soccer tournament

amateur Someone who does something without pay

assist A play, such as a pass, that sets up a goal-scoring opportunity

attack In soccer, any attempt to score a goal or create an opportunity to score a goal

cerebral palsy A physical condition that causes difficulty in body movement

chaotic When there is no order or rules, causing a lot of confusion

colonists People who leave their country and move to live in another country, bringing their rules and way of life with them

continental confederation An organization of the national soccer associations on one continent

corner kick A kick taken from the corner of the field by an attacking player when a defending player kicks the ball out of bounds beside their net

federation A collection of organizations that work together

governing body A group of people who are responsible for controlling how an organization is run

improvise To make something from materials not intended for that purpose

league A group of clubs that play against one another

marksmen People who aim at and shoot a target well

munitions Materials used for war, such as weapons

muscular impairment A disability relating to muscles or movement

offside A player who is closer to the opposing team's goal line than the ball or a player from the opposing team

professional Someone who is paid for what he or she does

qualifying event A game or series of games that is played to determine who will move on to another tournament

quarter-final A series of four games played by the top eight teams in a tournament

rebound In soccer, a rebound is when the ball bounces off something or someone and the ball is still in play

rugby A game related to soccer, in which players are allowed to use their hands

semi-final A series of two games played by the top four teams in a tournament

tackle In soccer, to attempt to gain possession of the ball from another player

throw-ins In soccer, a throw-in restarts the game after the ball goes out of bounds

versatile Able to adapt quickly and be effective in many ways

visually impaired Describes a condition of limited or no eyesight

LEARNING MORE

Check out these books and websites to learn more about soccer.

Books

Everything You Need to Know About Soccer! DK Children, 2024.

Greenberg, Keith Elliot. *US National Soccer Teams: Ultimate Fan Guide.* Lerner, 2026.

Hunter, Nick. *The Story of Soccer.* Capstone Press, 2025.

Mugford, Simon. *Soccer Rules the World: Incredible Stories from the Biggest Game on the Planet.* Welbeck Children's Books, 2023.

Websites

www.fifa.com
The FIFA website provides information on upcoming events, including the Olympics and World and Euro Cups. You can also watch live matches and test your soccer knowledge with trivia and other online games.

www.mlssoccer.com
The MLS website has all the latest news and videos of action in the men's league of North America.

www.nwslsoccer.com
The National Women's Soccer League website has match details, statistics, and player profiles of all your favorite players in the United States.

INDEX